1004 Salt & Pepper Shakers

Nursery Rhyme and Literary Characters

Larry Carey & Sylvia Tompkins

Schiffer Publishing Ltd

4880 Lower Valley Rd. Atglen, PA 19310 USA

Acknowledgments

We greatly appreciate the encouragement and assistance of fellow collectors, and especially the following contributors to this book: Gaye Adsett, Barb Era Beckey, Nancee Brewer, Carol and Ross Campbell, Diane Cauwels, Trish Claar, Frances Clements, Nigel Dalley, Marilyn DiPrima, Pat and Mike Disney, Jeanne Fouts, Dot Gammon, Shirley Gimondo, Lola Gonia, Marty Grossman, Lorraine Haywood, Jo Helmig, Betty and Freddie Hunter, Wendy R. Johnston, Heath Karr, Sharon and Ralph Karr, Marjorie Keiser, Gena and Jeff Kornblith, Jeanne Langer, Eric Lodge, Sandy Lyon, Phil Mays, Clara and Hubert McHugh, Rita Merrill, Jean Moon, Noreen Neary, Joyce and Bob Porter, Kathleen Pyle, Joanne Rose, Jean Rowe, Diana Sanderson, Kay M. Smith, Marcia Smith, Joan Szoc, Irene Thornburg, Laura and Carl Urban, Karen Weaver, Ruth Weeks, Ruth and Ken Wittlief, Betsy Zalewski, Sally Zenchenko.

Title page: 4.5". 1994. One of a kind set, created by Betty Harrington, formerly of Ceramic Arts Studio, Madison, WI. Sold at the Novelty Salt & Pepper Shakers Club Convention auction for $5000.

Library of Congress Catalog Card Number: 97-81443

Design by Bonnie M. Hensley
Layout by Randy L. Hensley & Jerry Fronefield
Pirinesi Lt BT/Futura Lt BT

ISBN: 0-7643-0553-0
Printed in China
1 2 3 4

Published by Schiffer Publishing Ltd.
4880 Lower Valley Road
Atglen, PA 19310
Phone: (610) 593-1777; Fax: (610) 593-2002
e-mail: schifferbk@aol.com
Please write for a free catalog.
This book may be purchased from the publisher.
Please include $3.95 for shipping.

Please try your bookstore first.

We are interested in hearing from authors
with book ideas on related subjects.

Collector/Club member Marjorie Keiser with Itzy resting in her favorite spot. Itzy thinks she is also a Club member as she's been to the last seven S&P conventions, traveling in her motorhome through 32 states to attend.

Introduction

This book covers nursery rhyme and literary characters, including children's stories and fables. This popular area of salt and pepper shakers appeals to a wide range of collecting interests. Licensing information is provided as marked on the sets. Some sets are subject to personal interpretation, influenced by the eye of the beholder.

Values are based upon our experience and input from contributors. They are intended as a guide only and will vary depending on condition, geographical area, knowledge of the seller or buyer, and to some extent, sheer luck.

In most cases the actual rhyme or a synopsis of the related story are provided. The characters are generally presented in alphabetical order of the associated reference.

The Novelty Salt & Pepper Shakers Club

The 1,600 members of the Novelty Salt & Pepper Shakers Club have discovered the enjoyment and benefit to be derived from joining with others who share a love for our hobby. Each year the Club convention is held in a different part of the country to afford the opportunity for attendance to as many members as possible. Our four annual newsletters provide information on shaker identification and history, as well as the chance to buy, sell, and trade. For more information about this Club, contact the authors.

Condiment with Little Boy Blue and Little Bo Peep. 2.25". 1996. Sandy Srp, OH, USA. $125.

Aladdin and his Lamp

4.5". 1960s. USA. Vallona Starr, CA. $60-65.

Aladdin in three different poses; each comes with lamp, one shown here. 4.25"-4.5". 1970s. Japan. Left set, harder to find, $28-30. Others, $22-25.

Mini. 1.25". 1960s. Arcadia Ceramics, CA, USA, $75-80.

4.25". 1960s. USA. Above: $30-35, right: $40-45.

3.25". 1960s. Poinsettia Studios, CA, USA. $80-85.

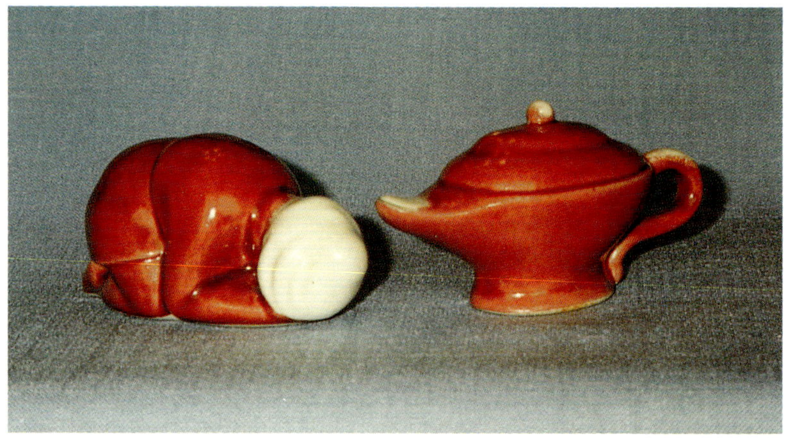

1.75". 1960s. USA. $18-20.

Baa Baa Black Sheep

Baa, baa, black sheep,
Have you any wool?
Yes, sir, yes, sir,
Three bags full;
One for the master,
And one for the dame,
And one for the little boy
Who lives down the lane.

2.5". 1960s. USA. $40-45.

Stacker. 4.5". 1960s. Japan. $40-45.

Babar

Babar is the hero of French stories written by Jean de Brunhoff in the early 1900s. He went to live with a kind old lady in the city after his mother was killed by a hunter. Returning to the forest, he was elected King of the elephants.

3.5". 1960s. Japan. $40-45.

Barber Shaving the Pig

Barber, barber, shave a pig,
How many hairs will make a wig?
Four and twenty, that's enough.
Give the barber a pinch of snuff.

3.25". 1960s. Japan. $35-40.

The Bible

Garden of Eden

Temptation. 4". 1990s, Clay Art, Philippines. $18-20.

Snake and apple. 2.5". 1960s. USA. $25-28.

Jonah and the Whale

2.25". 1960s. Japan. Note difference in Jonahs and whales. $40-45.

3.5". 1950s. Japan. $40-45.

The Last Supper

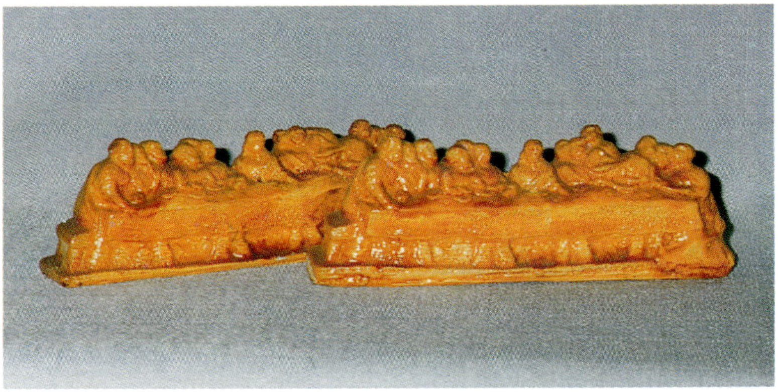

1.5". 1950s. Chalk. USA. $20-22.

1.75". 1950s. One piece chalk. USA. $30-35.

Noah's Ark

Condiment. 3". 1930s. Germany. Note, giraffe's head is spoon. $150-175.

Condiment. 3.5". 1960s. Japan. Enesco. $35-40.

3". 1960s. USA. $35-40.

3.75". 1990s. China. $10-12.

5.5". 1990s. China. Omnibus. $15-18.

3.25". 1990s. China. Youngs. $8-10.

4.25". 1990s. China. Front and back views. $12-15.

3". 1990s. China. CIC. $15-18.

2.5". 1990s. China. $8-10.

The Lion and the Lamb. 2.75". 1950s. Meridan, USA. $40-45.

Lot and his wife. 3.25". 1970s. Private ceramicist. USA. $30-35.

Jesus and the Devil. 4.25". © 1984, Richard Keenan, USA. $30-35.

Captain Ahab and Moby Dick. 3". 1950s. USA. Metal. $18-20.

The Cat in the Hat

by Dr. Seuss

7.25". 1996. USA. Private ceramicist. $125-150.

7.25". 1996. USA. Private ceramicist. Sold at Novelty S&P Shakers Club Convention Auction for $600.

Church Mouse. 3". 1960s. USA. $20-22.

Curious George

H.A. Rey wrote a story about a happy monkey named George who lived in Africa. He had but one fault: he was too curious.

One day George saw a man with a large yellow hat. When the man put his hat on the ground, George was curious and came down from the tree to look at it. George picked up the hat and put it on, but as it covered his head, he couldn't see. The man picked him up, put him in a bag and took him on a boat to a big zoo.

3.5". 1990s. China. Vandor. Licensed by Universal Studios Licensing, Inc. $16-18.

Cupid. 2". 1950s. M. Weese. USA. $50-60.

Charles Dickens

The shakers on this page are Charles Dickens characters sold as mix or match sets. Each set must be comprised of two shakers from the same country of origin. 2.75-3". 1930s & 1940s. Czechoslovakia sets $30-35; Germany sets $40-45. Goebel sets $50-55.

Mr. Pickwick from *Pickwick Papers*, Germany & Goebel.

Mrs. Gamp (Sairey Gamp), a fat midwife from *The Life and Adventure of Martin Chuzzlewit*, Germany, Erphila Czechoslovakia, Goebel.

Sam Weller from *Pickwick Papers*, Germany, Erphila Czechoslovakia, Goebel.

Bumble, a beadle (boy's home officer) from *Oliver Twist*, Germany.

All Goebel.

Mr. Pickwick condiments. 3.5". Germany. 1957. Goebel. $250+.

Mr. Pickwick condiment. 3.5". Germany. 1930s. $150+.

Sam Weller condiment. 3.5". Germany. 1930s. $150+.

Sairey Gamp condiment. 3.5". Germany. 1930s. $150+.

Sam Weller and Sairey Gamp. 2.5". 1950s. Japan. $25-30.

Mr. Micawber & Sairey Gamp

3.5". 1970s. England. Beswick. $40-45.

All the following are: 3". 1960s. Japan. $8-10.

The following are 3", 1960s, Artone, England, $40-45.

Dickens characters. He is imprinted Mr. ? Names are illegible.

Mr. Pickwick & Little Nell.

Sam Weller & Bumble.

Bill Sykes & Mr. Pickwick.

Cap'n Cuttle from *Dombey and Sons*, and Mr. Pickwick.

Sam Weller and Mr. Pickwick. 2.25". 1950s. Japan. $12-15.

Scrooge. 3.5". 1990s. Fitz & Floyd. China. $30-35.

Mr. Pickwick & Parson Brown. 2.5". 1950s. Japan. $12-15.

Mr. Micawber & Sam Weller. 3". 1950s. Marked Foreign. $40-45.

Farmer Giles & Sairey Gamp. 2.5". 1950s. Japan. $12-15.

Mr. Pickwick. 3". 1950s. Japan. $20-25.

Elves & Fairies

5.5". 1950s. Germany. $90-100.

4.5". 1960s. Napco. Japan. $15-18.

Condiment. 3". 1960s. Shafford. Japan. $45-50.

Condiment. 2.5". 1950s. Japan. $65-70.

3.75". 1950s. Japan. $15-18.

4". 1960s. Shafford. Japan. $35-40.

4". 1960s. Japan. $12-15.

4.25". 1980s. Japan. Napco Originals by Giftcraft. $35-40.

Fairy on stump house. 4". 1960s. Japan. $20-22.

Condiment. 3". 1950s. Japan. $65-70.

Father Time. 4". 1950s. USA. $30-35.

The Fox and the Goose

The Fox's Foray

A fox jumped up one winter's night,
And begged the moon to give him light,
For he'd many miles to trot that night
Before he reached his den O!

The first place he came to was a farmer's yard,
Where the ducks and the geese declared it hard
That their nerves should be shaken and their rest so marred
By a visit from Mr. Fox O!

He took the grey goose by the neck,
And swung him right across his back;
The grey goose cried out, Quack, quack, quack,
With his legs hanging dangling down O!

Old Mother Slipper Slopper jumped out of bed,
And out of the window she popped her head:
Oh! John, John, John, the grey goose is gone,
And the fox is off to his den O!

The fox went back to his hungry den,
And his dear little foxes, eight, nine, ten;
Quoth they, Good daddy, you must go there again,
If you bring such good cheer from the farm O!

The fox and his wife, without any strife,
Said they never ate a better goose in all their life:
They did very well without fork or knife,
And the little ones picked the bones O!

Condiment. 3". 1950s. Germany. Goebel. $175+.

3". 1950s. USA. Ceramic Arts Studio. $150-175.

The Fox and the Grapes

(Aesop's Fable)

A hungry Fox happened to be passing along a Vineyard where many fine bunches of grapes were hanging high on the arbor. The Fox leaped to get some, time and time again. Failing to do so and weary with jumping, he finally gave up, and as he trotted away he said to himself, "I didn't want them anyway; I know they must still be sour."

2.5". 1980s. Ron Gordon Designs, Inc. Japan. $18-20.

4". 1950s. USA. $35-40.

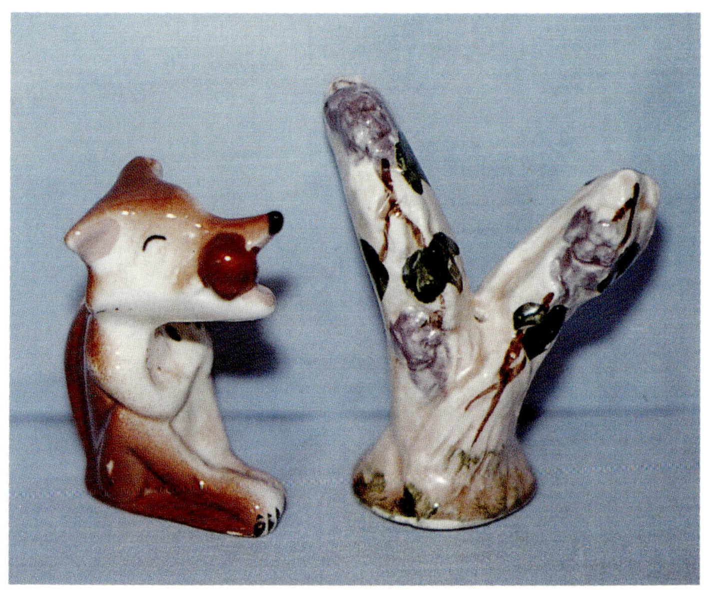

2.75". 1950s. USA. $35-40.

Genie on "magic carpet". 3"-4". 1960s. Japan. $15-18.

Georgie Porgie

Georgie Porgie, pudding and pie,
Kissed the girls and made them cry;
When the boys came out to play,
Georgie Porgie ran away.

3.5". 1986. Taiwan. Mother Goose series by Shafford. © Tempest Co. $35-40.

Gingham Dog and Calico Cat

The Duel by Eugene Field

The gingham dog and the calico cat
Side by side on the table sat;
'Twas half-past 12, and (what do you think!)
Nor one nor t'other had slept a wink!
The old Dutch clock and the Chinese plate
Appeared to know as sure as fate
There was going to be a terrible spat.
(I wasn't there; I simply state
What was told to me by the Chinese plate!)

The gingham dog went "bow-wow-wow!"
And the calico cat replied "mee-ow!"
The air was littered, an hour or so,
With bits of gingham and calico.
While the old Dutch clock in the chimney-place
Up with its hand before its face,
For it always dreaded a family row!
(Now mind: I'm only telling you
What the old Dutch clock declares is true!)

The Chinese plate looked very blue,
And wailed, "Oh dear! What shall we do?"
But the gingham dog and the calico cat
Wallowed this way and tumbled that,
Employing every tooth and claw
In the awfullest way you ever saw—
And, oh! How the gingham and calico flew!
(Don't fancy I exaggerate—
I got my news from the Chinese plate!)

Next morning, where the two had sat
They found no trace of dog or cat;
And some folks think unto this day
That burglars stole that pair away!
But the truth about the cat and pup
Is this: They ate each other up!
Now what do you really think of that?
(The old Dutch clock it told me so,
And that is how I came to know.)

4". 1960s. Brayton Laguna Pottery. USA. $45-50.

3". 1950s. Ceramic Arts Studio. USA. $55-60.

3". 1950s. Vallona Starr, USA. $70-75.

3". 1960s. PY, Napco. Japan. $35-40.

3.25". 1960s. Japan. $20-22.

Goldilocks and the Three Bears

Once upon a time there were three bears who lived in a house in the wood. One was a Little Wee Bear, one a Middle-sized Bear, and the other a Great Big Bear. They each had a bowl for porridge, a chair to sit in, and a bed to sleep in. One day while they were out, a little girl named Goldilocks came in and sampled their porridge, tried out the chairs and the beds, and was found asleep in the Wee Bear's bed when the Bears returned.

Mama and Papa are one shaker, baby is the other. 4.5". 1960s. Japan. $90-100.

One, three, and four holes. 4.25". 1950s. England. $125-150.

3.5". 1970s. Japan. $30-35.

Mama and Papa Bear. 3.5". 1950s. Japan. $35-40.

4". 1960s. Regal China. USA. $125-150.

4.5". 1960s. Regal china, No 54161, USA. $125-150.

3". 1990s. Taiwan. Applause. $12-15.

Golliwogs

In 1895 Florence Upton, an English artist, was looking for a new way to illustrate her children's books. She found a black-faced rag doll she called a golliwog, or golly, which became a hit in her books. Subsequently gollies were produced in a variety of forms.

3". 1990s. Zoom, England. $125-150.

3.75". 1980s. Silver Crane Co. England. $150-175.

3". 1950s. Japan. $150-175.

Goose Girl. 3.75". 1950s. Japan. $55-60.

The Hare and the Tortoise

(Aesop's Fable)

A Hare was once boasting about how fast he could run when a Tortoise, overhearing him, said, "I'll run you a race." "Done," said the Hare and laughed to himself; "but let's get the Fox for a judge." The Fox consented and the two started. The Hare quickly outran the Tortoise, and knowing he was far ahead, lay down to take a nap. "I can soon pass the Tortoise whenever I awaken." But unfortunately, the Hare overslept; and when he awoke, though he ran his best, he found the Tortoise was already at the goal. He had learned that "Slow and steady wins the race."

2.5". 1960s. Japan. $12-15.

2.75". 1960s. Vallona Starr. USA. Left set, harder to find, $60-65. Right; $32-35.

3.25". 1960s. New England Ceramics. USA. $18-20.

3.5". 1950s. Poinsettia Studios. USA. $80-85.

2.5". 1960s. Japan. $12-15.

1.5". 1960s. Japan. $12-15.

2.5". 1950s. Japan. Left set: $12-15.
Other sets: $22-25.

3". 1990s. China. Strata Group. $12-15.

Mini. 1.5". 1950s. USA. $25-30.

2.5". 1990s. China. Albert Price Products. $8-10.

1". 1960s. USA. William H. Hirsch Mfg. Co., Los Angeles, CA. $18-20.

3.25". 1980s. Taiwan. Fitz & Floyd. $40-45.

Shown out of box.

2.5". 1970s. France. $55-60.

Hansel & Gretel

(Grimm's Fairy Tale)

Hansel and Gretel lived with their father, a poor woodcutter, and stepmother in a forest. As times were hard, the stepmother convinced the father to take the children deep into the forest and abandon them. Lost, they came upon a witch's gingerbread house. The witch planned to eat them but instead was herself killed. Finding many jewels, the children returned home with them to find their stepmother gone and their father delighted to see them.

Shown kissing and apart. 4.25". 1950s. Japan. Copyright 1954, Michael Myersberg Productions. $25-30.

5.5". 1990s. USA. Rick Wisecarver, OH. $50-55.

Condiments. 3.25". 1950s. Japan. $65-70.

Hey Diddle Diddle

Hey Diddle Diddle
The Cat and the Fiddle
The Cow Jumped over the Moon
The little Dog laughed
To see such sport
And the Dish ran away with the Spoon.

4.25". 1960s. Probably New England Ceramics. USA. $20-22.

3.5". 1950s. USA. $30-35.

2.5". 1950s. USA. $18-20.

4". 1950s. Japan. $22-25.

4". 1950s. USA. $18-20.

3.25"-3.5". 1950s. USA. $18-20.

The Cat fits the Fiddle. 3.25". 1960s. Japan. $25-30.

2.5". 1960s. Japan. $25-30.

2". 1960s. Japan. $22-25.

2.75". 1980s. Josef Originals. Korea. $70-75.

4". 1990s. China. Enesco, issued with moon Cookie Jar. $15-18.

3.5". 1960s. Probably New England Ceramics. USA. $20-22.

3.25". 1960s. USA. $30-35.

3.25". 1960s. Private ceramicist. USA. $10-12.

3.5". 1970s. USA. $12-15.

3.25". 1990s. © Susan Winget, CIC, Thailand. $12-15.

3.25"-3.5". 1960s.
USA. $15-18.

4". 1990s. Philippines. Clay Art.
$18-20.

3". 1960s. Left, USA. Right, Japan. $18-20.

3.75". 1990s. Strata Group, Philippines. $18-20.

3.75". 1950s. USA. © NEC. $40-45.

Hickory, Dickory, Dock

Hickory, dickory, dock,
The mouse ran up the clock;
The clock struck one,
The mouse ran down—
Hickory, dickory, dock.

2.75". 1950s. USA. $12-15.

5". 1960s. Probably N.E. Ceramics. USA. $15-18.

3". 1960s. Japan. Lefton China. $18-20.

House of Seven Gables. 1.5". 1950s. Private ceramicist, USA. $18-20.

Humpty Dumpty

Humpty Dumpty sat on a wall.
Humpty Dumpty had a great fall.
All the King's horses
And all the King's men
Couldn't put Humpty together again.

Note: Included are sets identified as Humpty Dumpty and egghead people only if they are on walls.

Condiment. 2.5". 1950s. Foreign (Japan). $80-85.

Condiment. 4". 1950s. Japan. Note: Green hat is end of spoon. $70-75.

Humpty and Mrs. Dumpty. 4.75"-7.5". 1950s. Japan. Tiliso. Small set, $25-30. Large, $45-50.

4.5". 1960s. Regal China, USA. $90-100.

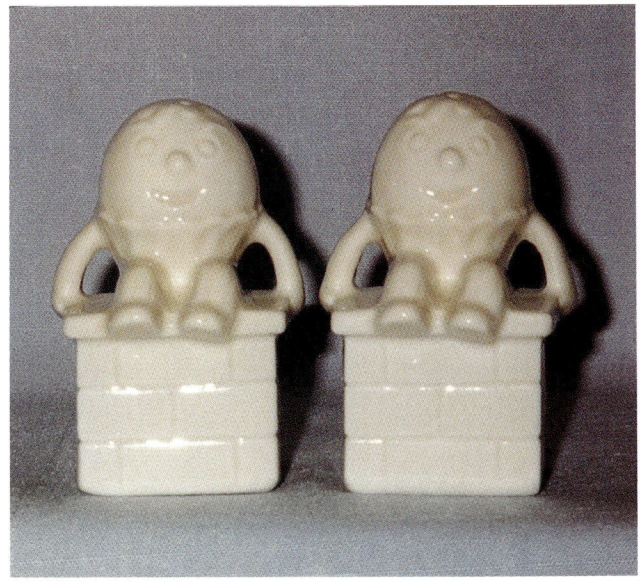

4.5". 1960s. Unpainted Regal China. USA. $125-135.

Four piece. 4". 1970s. Tony Wood Studio, England. Note: Faces professionally added to original set. $100-110.

Humpty Dumpty & Old Woman in the Shoe. 2.25"-2.75". 1960s. Japan. $20-25.

Three piece small set. 3". Four piece large set (heads are S&P) 5.75". 1950s. Ardalt. Japan. Small, $25-30. Large, $85-90.

Three piece. 3.5". 1950s. Ardalt. Occupied Japan. $55-60.

4.25". 1960s. Japan. $45-50.

Three piece. 3". 1950s. Staffordshire-Morley, England. $60-65.

Three piece. 3". 1950s. Thorley Bone China, England. $60-65.

Three piece. 3.25". 1950s. Japan. $18-20.

3.5". 1950s. Probably USA. $15-18.

3 piece. 3.75". 1940s. Occupied Japan. Original price, 98 cents. $18-20.

Three piece. 3"-3.5". 1970s. Private ceramicist, USA. $12-15.

3.75". 1960s. Japan. $40-45.

2.25". 1950s. England. $45-50.

2.5". 1950s. England. $45-50.

3". 1950s. USA. $18-20.

3.75". 1950s. USA. $30-35.

2.5"-3.25". 1950s. Japan. $10-12.

3.25". 1950s. USA. $22-25.

2.5". 1950s. Japan. $12-15.

4.75". 1950s. England. $90-100.

3". 1980s. Josef Originals. Korea. $70-75.

3". 1950s. M. Weese, USA. $50-60.

4.5". 1990s. Philippines. Clay Art. $20-22.

3.25". 1950s. USA. $10-12 set.

4.25". 1950s. Urda, USA. $40-45.

5.25". 1950s. Leyden Arts, CA. USA. $35-40.

4.5". 1950s. USA. $30-35.

4.75". 1950s. USA. $25-30.

4.25". 1990s. Albert E. Price, China. $8-10.

3.75". 1990s. Norcrest, Korea. $10-12.

Probably egg cup tops. Front and back views. 2.5". 1960s. Japan. $12-15.

Mini. 1.75". 1990s. Sandy Srp, OH. $50-60.

3". 1980s. Left set: Taiwan. Lefton. $12-15. Right set: Hong Kong. Plastic. $8-10.

2.25". 1950s. USA.
Gold trim, $20-22.
Others, $15-18.

3.75". 1990s. Indonesia.
Omnibus. $20-25.

2.5". 1950s. Japan. $15-18.

Three piece. 4". 1980s.
Smiles, Japan. $8-10.

3.25". 1990s. Midwest of Cannon Falls, MN. Taiwan.
$12-15.

4". 1990s. China. Enesco, issued with matching cookie jar. $15-18.

4.25". 1950s. USA. Patent No. 156848. $15-18.

Shown as originally sold with napkin holder and original box. Usually found as only S&P in colors shown. Note: Hats are stoppers. 3". 1950s. USA. S&P only, $12-15. Complete set, $22-25.

Three piece plastic. 3". 1980s. Hong Kong. © JSNY. $8-10.

1.75"-2.25". 1950s. USA.
Chalkware. $8-10.

3.25". 1950s. USA.
Wood. $8-10.

Jack and Jill

Jack and Jill went up the hill
To fetch a pail of water;
Jack fell down and broke his crown,
And Jill came tumbling after.

Up Jack got, and home did trot
As fast as he could caper;
Went to bed to mend his head,
With vinegar and brown paper.

2.75". 1980s. Josef Originals. Korea. $70-75.

3.5". 1960s. Japan. $25-30.

4". 1960s. Japan. Also belongs to a series of people from various countries. $20-22.

Jack and Jill and Little Boy Blue. 3.25". 1930s. Germany. Royal Bayreuth. $200+.

3.5". 1950s. Japan. $18-20.

3.25". 1960s. Japan. $18-20.

1.75". 1960s. Japan. $35-40.

4". 1950s. Japan. $12-15.

4". 1950s. USA. $70-75.

3". 1950s. M. Weese, USA. $50-60.

4". 1950s. Japan. $25-30.

4". 1950s. USA. $30-35.

1.75". 1950s. USA. Chalkware. $30-35.

Jack Be Nimble

Jack be nimble,
Jack be quick,
Jack jump over the candlestick.

3.75". 1960s. USA. $40-45.

Jack Sprat

Jack Sprat could eat no fat,
His wife could eat no lean;
And so, between them both, you see,
They licked the platter clean.

3.75". 1950s. Japan. $35-40.

King Midas

(from Greek mythology)

King Midas was a kind but rather stupid man who had always been a friend to the satyrs. Midas had spared from punishment an old satyr found sleeping in a favorite flower bed. This old satyr was a follower of Dionysus, and the god had rewarded Midas for his kindness by granting him the wish that everything he touched would turn to gold, making him the richest man on earth. But since even his food, drink, and little daughter turned into gold, Midas had to beg Dionysus to undo his wish and make everything as it had been before.

3.5". 1950s. Poinsettia Studios, USA. $80-85.

Kappa

The Kappa is the elfin watersprite of Japanese folklore and a dweller of the same fanciful realm as the Irish Leprechaun. His home is the misty wonderland of babbling brooks and swaying waterlilies. Kappa's charm must be refreshed by gentle dewdrops which cling to his bonnet of leaves. The magic hours of dawn and dusk are his time for frolic in our world.

Though his size is small, Kappa's strength is of legendary greatness and enables him to engage in his favorite pastime of Japanese Sumo wrestling, a sport in which this tiny marvel has no match. If one listens closely during the time when Kappa roams about, he can hear Kappa's magical challenge, "Try your luck against tiny Kappa."

Though Kappa can bind you in his spell, he is a lovable elf and his presence will bring everlasting joy and luck to the person who gazes upon his image. Cherish Kappa and the ageless charm of this sprite will be yours forever.

3.75". 1960s. Japan. A Quality Product. $35-40.

The Knight and the Dragon

3.75". 1950s. M. Weese, USA. $50-60.

Mini. 2". 1950s. Arcadia Ceramics, CA. $75-80.

3.25". 1990s. China. Albert E. Price Co. $8-10.

Ladybug

Ladybug, Ladybug
Fly away home
Your house is on fire
Your children will burn.
All but one whose name is Ann,
And she crept under the pudding pan.

Chinese version:

Ladybug, ladybug,
Fly away, do
Fly to the mountain,
And feed upon dew,
Feed upon dew
And sleep on a rug,
And then run away
Like a good little bug.

3.25". 1950s. Probably USA. $15-18.

2". 1950s. Vallona Starr, USA. $60-65.

3". 1960s. Japan. $20-25.

2.5". 1950s. Japan. $12-15.

3.25". 1950s. Japan. $12-15.

10.5". 1960s. Japan. $20-25.

Top set, 2.5"; bottom, 1.5". 1950s. Japan. $10-12.

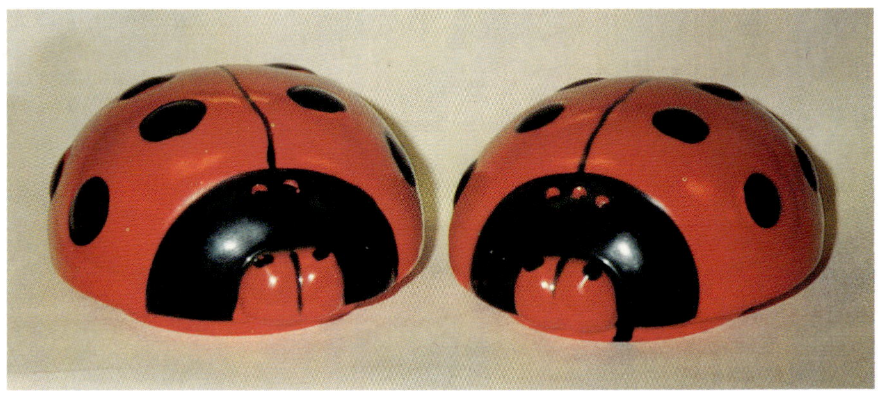

2.5" h., 5.5" l. 1950s. Japan. $15-18.

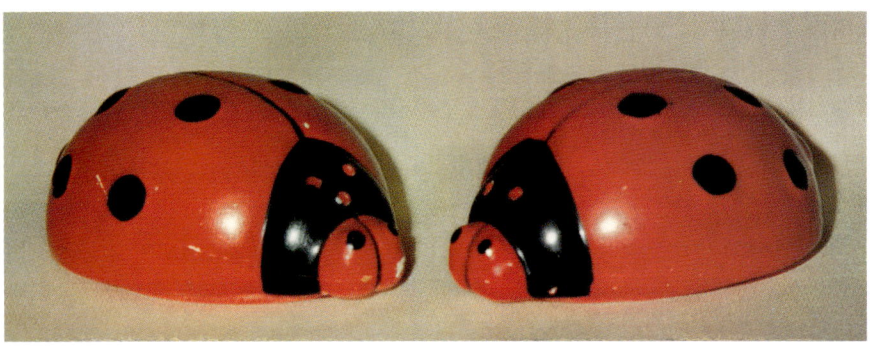

1.5". 1950s.
Japan. $10-12.

2.5". 1950s. Probably USA. Note separate wings. $12-15.

2.25". 1950s. Japan. Composition material. $5-8.

3". 1960s. Japan. $10-12.

3.5". 1960s. Japan. $15-18.

Leprechauns

3.5". 1990s. Sri Lanka. Omnibus. $15-18.

"Shaughnessy's Little People," 4.25". 1989. Taiwan. Fitz and Floyd. $55-60.

2.75". 1970s. Japan. $22-25.

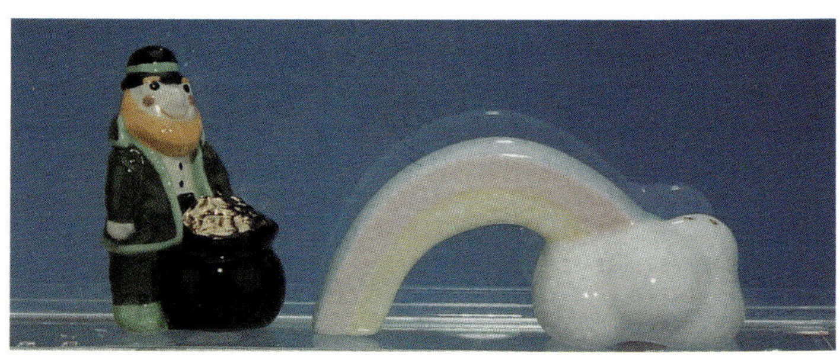

1.25". 1990s. USA. Sandy Srp. $50-60.

3.5". 1960s. Japan. $20-22.

3.25". 1990s. China. Russ Berrie & Co. $15-18.

2.5". 1990s. Indonesia. Enesco. $15-18.

The Lion and the Mouse

(Aesop's Fable)

A sleeping Lion was awakened by a Mouse running over his face. Losing his temper he seized it with his paw and was about to kill it. The Mouse, terrified, entreated him to spare its life and cried, "One day I will repay you for your kindness." The idea of so insignificant a creature being able to do anything for him amused the Lion so much that he let it go. But one day the Lion got entangled in a net. The Mouse recognized his roars of anger, ran to the spot and gnawed the rope with its teeth, setting the Lion free. "There!" said the Mouse, "you laughed at me when I promised I would repay you: but now you see, even a Mouse can help a Lion."

3.5". 1970s. Japan. $25-30.

2.5". 1960s. USA. $15-18.

Lion and crown (King of the Jungle). 1.75". 1950s. USA. $30-35.

Little Black Sambo

(Children's Book)

3.25". 1950s. USA. Ceramic Arts Studio. $400+.

Shown with clothes and after the tiger took them. 2.75". 1950s. Probably USA. $175+.

Shown apart and together. 5". 1990s. USA. The New Rose Collection, IL. $45-50.

Little Bo Peep

Little Bo-peep has lost her sheep,
And can't tell where to find them;
Leave them alone, and they'll come home,
Wagging their tails behind them.

Little Bo-peep fell fast asleep,
And dreamt she heard them bleating;
But when she awoke, she found it a joke.
For they were still all fleeting.

Then up she took her little crook,
Determined for to find them;
She found them indeed, but it made her heart bleed,
For they'd left their tails behind them!

It happened one day, as Bo-peep did stray
Unto a meadow hard by—
That she espied their tails side by side,
All hung on a tree to dry.

She heaved a sigh and wiped her eye,
Then went over hill and dale,
And tried what she could, as a shepherdess should,
To tack to each sheep its tail.

Little Bo Peep and Little Miss Muffett, possibly singles. 3". 1950s. USA. $35-40.

Condiments. 3.75"-4.5". 1950s. Japan. Original price shown on one, $1.19. $65-70.

2.25". 1950s. Francis Fayre, England. $40-45.

3.5". 1980s. Josef Originals, Korea. $70-75.

5". 1970s. Private ceramicist, USA. $20-25.

4". 1950s. Japan. $20-22.

Little Boy Blue

Little Boy Blue,
Come blow your horn,
The sheep's in the meadow,
The cow's in the corn.

Where is the boy
Who looks after the sheep?
He's under a haycock
Fast asleep.

Will you wake him?
No, not I,
For if I do,
He's sure to cry.

Condiments. 3.75". 1950s. Japan. $80-90.

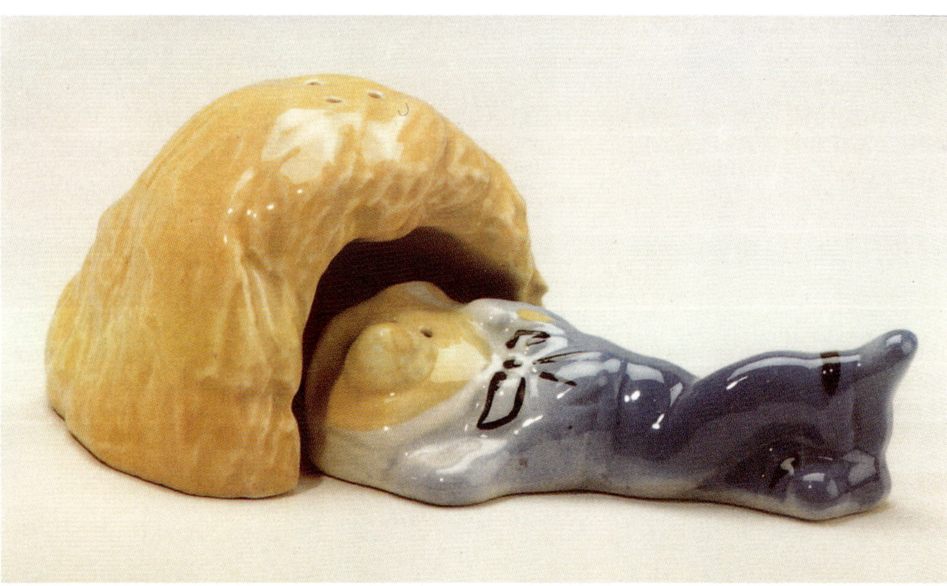

2.25". 1950s. Probably NEC, USA. $45-50.

Little Boy Blue and Little Bo Peep. 3.75". 1950s. Sorcha Boru, USA. $70-75.

3.75". 1950s. Japan. $25-30.

3". 1950s. Japan. $18-20.

2.5". 1950s. Japan. $85-90.

2". 1950s. England. $40-45.

2.5". 1950s. Shirley Ceramics, USA. Shown in three colors with bottom mark. $75-80.

The Little Engine that Could

by Watty Piper

A train filled with good things for children became disabled on the track. The engine asked the Shiny New Passenger Engine, the Big Strong Freight Engine, and the Rusty Old Engine to help in getting the train over the mountain to the children. They all refused. But the Little Blue Engine agreed to try, puffing "I think I can" and made it over the mountain, chugging, "I thought I could."

2". 1950s. Poinsettia Studios. $80-90.

2". 1950s. Japan. $30-35.

Little Jack Horner

Little Jack Horner
Sat in a corner,
Eating a Christmas pie;
He put in his thumb,
And took out a plum,
And said, "What a good boy am I!"

3.5". 1960s. USA. $40-45.

Little Miss Muffet

Little Miss Muffet
Sat on a tuffet,
Eating her curds and whey;
There came a big spider,
Who sat down beside her
And frightened Miss Muffet away.

3". 1950s. Vallona Starr, USA. $70-75.

4.25". 1950s. Ceramic Arts Studio, USA. $150+.

3.25". 1950s. USA. $40-45.

Little Miss Muffet and Little Jack Horner. 4.25". 1970s. Private ceramicist, USA. $45-50.

2.75". 1980s. Josef Originals, Korea. $70-75.

3.5". 1960s. Ucago, Japan. $30-35.

The Little Red Hen and the Grain of Wheat

A pig, a duck, a mouse, and a little red hen with her chicks all lived together. All the work of the house was left to the little red hen.

One day the little red hen found some grains of wheat.
"Who will help me sow the wheat?" she asked.
"Not I," said the pig.
"Not I," said the duck.
"Not I," said the mouse.
"Then I'll sow it myself," said the little red hen.

When the grain was tall, the little red hen asked,
"Who will help me cut the wheat?"
"Not I," said the pig.
"Not I," said the duck.
"Not I," said the mouse.
"Then I'll cut it myself," said the little red hen.

"Who will help me carry the grain to the mill?"
"Not I," said the pig.
"Not I," said the duck.
"Not I," said the mouse.
"Then I'll carry it myself," said the little red hen.

"Who will help me bake the bread?"
"Not I," said the pig.
"Not I," said the duck.
"Not I," said the mouse.
"Then I'll bake it myself," said the little red hen.

When the bread was baked, she asked,
"Who will come and help me eat?"
"I will," grunted the pig.
"I will," quacked the duck.
"I will," squeaked the mouse.

"No you won't! I'll do it myself," said the little red hen. And she called all her little chicks together and they ate up the bread to the very last crumb.

Nursery Rhyme:

I had a little hen, the prettiest ever seen;
She washed me the dishes, and kept the house clean;
She went to the mill to fetch me some flour.
She brought it home in less than an hour;
She baked me my bread, she brewed me my ale,
She sat by the fire and told many a fine tale.

3.5". 1950s. Poinsettia Studios, USA. $80-85.

Little Red Riding-Hood

There was once upon a time a little village girl, the prettiest ever seen or known, of whom her mother was dotingly fond. Her grandmother was even fonder of her still, and had a little red hood made for the child, which suited her so well that wherever she went she was known by the name of Little Red Riding-Hood.

Unpainted small set. $55-60.

Left set, 5". Right, 3.25". 1960s. Hull Pottery, USA. Shown in one of many design variations. Also produced in rare 4" size. Left, $90-100; right, $40-50.

4.5". 1960s. Kass, USA. Shown with and without trim. $75-80

3". 1970s. Private ceramicist, USA. $30-35.

4.5". 1950s. USA. $28-30.

3". 1950s. USA. $25-28.

2.25". 1950s.
England. $40-45.

4.5". 1950s. USA. $25-28.

Stacker. 3.5". 1960s. USA. $70-75.

5.25"-6". 1990s. USA. Rick Wisecarver. $50-55.

4". 1960s. Japan. $90-100.

3.75". 1950s. Poinsettia Studios, USA. $70-75.

3.5". 1950s. Japan. $25-30.

3.5". 1990s. Philippines. Clay Art. $18-20.

3.25". 1930s. Germany. Sets sold two ways as shown. Right, $70-75. Below, $55-60.

The Man in the Moon

(three different rhymes)

The Man in the Moon was caught
in a trap
For stealing the thorns from another
man's gap.
If he had gone by, and let the thorns
lie,
He'd never been Man in the Moon
so high.

The man in the moon
Came down too soon,
And asked his way to Norwich;
He went by the south,
And burnt his mouth
With supping cold plum porridge.

The man in the moon drinks claret,
But he is a dull jack-a-dandy;
Would he know a sheep's head from
a carrot,
He should learn to drink cider and
brandy.

3.5". 1950s. Probably USA. $100-110.

Stacker. 3.5"-4.25". 1950s.
Japan. $90-100.

Mary Had a Little Lamb

Mary had a little lamb,
Its fleece was white as snow,
And every where that Mary went
The lamb was sure to go.

It followed her to school one day,
Which was against the rule.
It made the children laugh and play
To see a lamb at school.

And so the teacher turned it out,
But still it lingered near,
And waited patiently about
Till Mary did appear.

And then it ran to her and laid
Its head upon her arm,
As if it said, "I'm not afraid—
You'll keep me from all harm."

"What makes the lamb love Mary so?"
The eager children cry.
"Why, Mary loves the lamb,
you know,"
The teacher did reply.

4". 1960s. Japan. $50-60.

3.75". 1960s. Regal China. USA. © Van Tellingen. $30-35 set.

3". 1950s. Japan. $18-20.

3.5". 1960s. Japan. Enesco. Note: Color of ribbon on lamb matches dress. $30-35.

2.75". 1950s. M.Weese, USA. $50-60.

4". 1960s. Japan. Tag says "Mary & her Little Lamb". $25-30.

2.75"-3.25". 1950s. Japan.
Comes in several sizes.
$12-15.

4". 1960s.
Meridan, USA.
$40-45.

2.75". 1950s. USA. Chalkware.
$12-15.

3.25". 1950s. USA.
$22-25.

3.5". 1950s.
Japan. $15-18.

3.25". 1950s. USA. $20-25.

3.25". 1950s. USA. Label says "Made in California for Gimbels." $20-25.

Mary, Mary

Mary, Mary, quite contrary,
How does your garden grow?
With silver bells and cockle shells
And pretty maids all in a row.

3". 1950s. Japan. $25-30.

3.25". 1950s. © Shirley Ceramics, USA. $75-80

4.25". 1950s. Sorcha Boru, USA. $70-75.

Moth and the Flame. 2". 1950s. Gimbels, USA. $22-25.

Old Mother Goose and the Golden Egg

Old Mother Goose,
When she wanted to wander,
Would ride through the air
On a very fine gander.

Mother Goose had a house,
'Twas built in a wood,
Where an owl at the door
For sentinel stood.

She had a son Jack,
A plain-looking lad,
He was not very good,
Nor yet very bad.

She sent him to market,
A live goose he bought;
See, mother, says he,
I have not been for naught.

Jack's goose and her gander
Grew very fond;
They'd both eat together,
Or swim in the pond.

Jack found one fine morning,
As I have been told,
His goose had laid him
An egg of pure gold.

Jack ran to his mother
The news for to tell,
She called him a good boy,
And said it was well.

Jack sold his gold egg
To a merchant untrue,
Who cheated him out of
A half of his due.

Then Jack went a-courting
A lady so gay,
As fair as the lily,
And sweet as the May.

The merchant and squire
Soon came at his back,
And began to belabour
The sides of poor Jack.

Then Old Mother Goose
That instant came in,
And turned her son Jack
Into famed Harlequin.

She then with her wand
Touched the lady so fine,
And turned her at once
Into sweet Columbine.

The gold egg in the sea
Was thrown away then,
When an odd fish brought her
The egg back again.

The merchant then vowed
The goose he would kill,
Resolving at once
His pockets to fill.

Jack's mother came in,
And caught the goose soon,
And mounting its back,
Flew up to the moon.

Mother Goose

Cackle, Cackle, Mother Goose,
Have you any feathers loose?
Truly, have I, pretty fellow,
Half enough to make a pillow.
And here are quills, take one or two,
And down to make a bed for you.

4". 1950s. USA. $65-75.

Condiment. 4.25". 1950s. Japan. Original cost, 49 cents. $90-100.

Condiments. 3.25". 1950s. Japan. $150-175.

Mother Goose and her son Jack, three piece sets. 3". 1940s. Marutomoware. Japan. $35-40.

5". 1950s. Japan. $25-30.

3.5". 1950s. Japan. $20-25.

Mother Goose and her son Jack. 3.75". 1950s. Japan. $22-25.

Three piece set. 3". 1940s. Japan. $35-40.

6". 1960s. USA. Twin Winton, CA. $35-40.

The Goose that Laid the Golden Egg

(Aesop's Fable)

One day a farmer went to the nest of his goose to see if she had laid an egg. To his great wonder and delight he found that instead of an ordinary egg, she had laid an egg of pure gold. He rushed to the house in great excitement to show his wife the treasure he had found and she too was overjoyed.

Every day thereafter the farmer visited the nest, and every day he found the goose had laid a beautiful glittering golden egg. The farmer took the eggs to market and soon began to get rich. But it was not long before he grew impatient with the goose because she gave him only a single golden egg a day. He was not getting rich quickly enough.

Then one day, after he had finished counting his money, the idea came to him that he could get all the golden treasure at once by killing the goose and cutting it open. But when the deed was done, not a single golden egg did he find, and his marvelous goose was dead.

The greedy who always want more often lose all.

4". 1960s. Left set: Vallona Starr. USA. $30-32. Right set: Japan. $15-18.

5.5". 1960s. USA. Vallona Starr. $30-32

4.75". 1960s. Japan. $15-18.

3.5". 1960s. USA.
$15-18.

4.5". 1960s. USA. $15-18.

4.75". 1960s. Japan. $12-15.

2.75". 1960s. USA. $12-15.

4". 1950s. Japan. $10-12.

3.5". 1970s. USA.
$25-30 set.

2.5". 1960s. Japan. $15-18.

4". 1950s. USA. $15-18.

3.5". 1960s. USA. Davis Products. $12-15.

2.75". 1960s. USA. $12-15.

3". 1950s. Japan. $10-12.

3.5". 1960s. USA. Davis Products. $10-12.

3.75". 1950s. Japan. $10-12.

3.75". 1960s. Japan. $12-15.

4". 1950s. Japan. © Holt Howard. $20-22.

2.25". 1950s. Japan. $10-12.

3.25". 1960s. Japan. $10-12.

Old King Cole

Old King Cole
Was a merry old soul.
And a merry old soul was he;
He called for his pipe
And he called for his bowl
And he called for his fiddlers three.
And every fiddler had a fine fiddle
And a very fine fiddle had he.
"Tweedle dee, tweedle dee, tweedle dee,"

2.75"-3.25". 1960s. Japan. $25-30.

4". 1950s. Japan. $25-30.

3.25". 1960s. Japan. $25-30.

3.25". 1960s. Japan. $25-30.

3.25". 1960s. USA. Note name on one chair. $45-50.

Stacker. 2.75". Bone china. England. $40-45.

3.75". 1960s. Japan. $30-35.

Old MacDonald

Farm couple. 4". 1960s. USA. Regal China. $70-75.

Churns. 4". 1960s. Regal China. USA. $55-60.

Feed sacks. 5". 1960s. Royal China. USA. Pat Pending. $90-100.

The Old Man and the Sea. 2.5". 1960s. USA. $30-35.

Old Mother Hubbard

Old Mother Hubbard
Went to the cupboard,
To fetch her poor dog a bone;
But when she came there
The cupboard was bare
And so the poor dog had none.

She went to the baker's
To buy him some bread;
But when she came back
The poor dog was dead.

She went to the undertaker's
To buy him a coffin;
But when she came back
The poor dog was laughing.

She took a clean dish
To get him some tripe;
But when she came back
He was smoking a pipe.

She went to the alehouse
To get him some beer;
But when she came back
The dog sat in a chair.

She went to the tavern
For white wine and red;
But when she came back
The dog stood on his head.

She went to the fruiterer's
To buy him some fruit;
But when she came back
He was playing the flute.

She went to the tailor's
To buy him a coat
But when she came back
He was riding a goat.

She went to the hatter's
To buy him a hat;
But when she came back
He was feeding the cat.

She went to the barber's
To buy him a wig;
But when she came back
He was dancing a jig.

She went to the cobbler's
To buy him some shoes;
But when she came back
He was reading the news.

She went to the seamstress
To buy him some linen;
But when she came back
The dog was a-spinning.

She went to the hosier's
To buy him some hose;
But when she came back
He was dressed in his clothes.

The dame made a curtsy,
The dog made a bow;
The dame said, Your servant,
The dog said, Bow-wow.

3.75". 1950s. Japan. $35-40.

The Twelve Days of Christmas (Partridge and Pear)

The first day of Christmas,
My true love sent to me
A partridge in a pear tree.

Partridge and pear. 3". 1991. Taiwan. Fitz & Floyd. $25-28.

Old Woman in the Shoe

There was an old woman
Who lived in a shoe.
She had so many children
She didn't know what to do.
She gave them some broth
Without any bread,
Then spanked them all soundly
And sent them to bed.

3.75". 1990s. Strata Group, Philippines. $15-18.

3.25". 1950s. Japan. $25-30.

2.25". 1950s. Francis Fayre, England. $40-45.

The Owl and the Pussy-Cat

by Edward Lear

The Owl and the Pussy-cat went to sea
In a beautiful pea-green boat;
They took some honey, and plenty of money
Wrapped up in a five-pound note.
The Owl looked up to the stars above,
And sang to a small guitar,
"O lovely Pussy, O Pussy, my love,
What a beautiful pussy you are,
You are,
You are—
What a beautiful pussy you are!"

Pussy said to the Owl, "You elegant fowl,
How charmingly sweet you sing!
Oh! let us be married; too long we have tarried
But what shall we do for a ring?"
They sailed away, for a year and a day,
To the land where the bong-tree grows;
And there in a wood a Piggy-wig stood,
With a ring at the end of his nose,
His nose,
His nose—
With a ring at the end of his nose.

"Dear Pig, are you willing to sell for one shilling
Your ring?" Said the Piggy, "I will."
So they took it away, and were married next day
By the turkey who lives on the hill.
They dined on mince and slices of quince,
Which they ate with a runcible spoon;
And hand in hand, on the edge of the sand,
They danced by the light of the moon,
The moon,
The moon—
They danced by the light of the moon.

3". 1950s. USA. $10-12.

3". 1980. Japan. Fitz & Floyd Inc. $65-70.

Pan

Pan. 3". 1950s. © USA. $50-60.

Pan. 3.5". 1950s. M. Weese, USA. $50-60.

Pease Porridge

Pease porridge hot,
Pease porridge cold,
Pease porridge in the pot
Nine days old.
Some like it hot,
Some like it cold,
Some like it in the pot
Nine days old.

3.75". 1950s.
Japan. $30-35.

Paul Bunyan and Babe

Paul Bunyan was a woodsman of great size and strength who was taller than the trees of the forest and who could take the tallest pine tree and break it in two with his bare hands.

One day when Paul was working in his father's logging camp in the Maine woods it snowed so that all but the tallest trees were buried, and the snow, instead of being white, was a bright sapphire blue!

When the snow stopped falling, Paul saw two little ears belonging to a baby ox calf sticking up through a snowdrift, so he took him home. He decided to call the little calf "Babe" and keep him for a pet. The strangest thing about Babe was that even after he thawed out his coat remained a soft glossy blue.

3". 1950s. M. Weese, USA. $50-60.

4". 1950s. Ceramic Arts Studio, USA. $125+.

3.5". 1960s. Victoria Ceramics, Japan. $18-20.

2.5". 1950s. Japan. $45-50.

2.25". 1950s. Rosemeade Pottery, USA. $90-100.

4". 1990s. China. Enesco. $15-18.

3". 1960s. Private ceramicist, USA. $15-18.

4.5". 1960s. Japan. $28-30.

4.25". 1950s. Japan. Composition material. $18-20.

5". 1970s. Japan. Composition material. $20-25.

4". 1960s. Japan. $20-25.

3.75". 1960s. Japan.
$28-30.

5.25". 1970s. Japan. $20-25.

4.25". 1970s. Japan.
$20-25.

3.75". 1980s. Taiwan. Composition material. $15-18.

4". 1960s. Japan.
$20-25.

4.5". 1960s. Japan. $20-25.

Peter, Peter

Peter, Peter, pumpkin eater,
Had a wife and couldn't keep her;
He put her in a pumpkin shell
And there he kept her very well.

Peter, Peter, pumpkin eater,
Had another, and didn't love her;
Peter learned to read and spell,
And then he loved her very well.

3.25". 1980s. Josef Originals, Korea. $70-75.

2.25". 1950s. Japan. Miyao. $25-30.

3.75". 1950s. Japan. $30-35.

3.5". 1950s. M. Weese, USA. $50-60.

4". 1990s. China. Enesco. Issued with Pumpkin Cookie Jar. $15-18.

2". 1950s. USA. Chalkware. $20-25.

Princess and the Frog

3.5". 1990s. Philippines. Clay Art. $18-20.

4". 1990s. Holland. Inspiration Holland. $12-15.

The Tale of Peter Rabbit

by Beatrix Potter

Once upon a time there were four little rabbits, and their names were Flopsy, Mopsy, Cotton-tail, and Peter. They lived with their mother in a sandbank, underneath the root of a very big fir tree.

"Now, my dears," said Mrs. Rabbit, "you may go into the fields or down the lane, but don't go into Mr. McGregor's garden." However, Peter was naughty and would sneak into the garden and eat the vegetables.

Benjamin Bunny is Peter's cousin and is married to Peter's sister Flopsy. In the book, Peter is always wearing an open blue jacket. The shaker is usually attired in an open blue coat.

4.5". 1990s. © Frederick Warne & Co. Malaysia. Enesco. $18-20.

Mother Rabbit with Peter, Flopsy, and Mopsy. 4". 1950s. Japan. Shafford. $20-25 set.

Peter Rabbit and Benjamin Bunny. 4". 1950s. Japan. $15-18.

Beatrix Potter Characters

Shown are unlicensed sets recognized as characters from her childrens' books.

Mice. 3". 1960s. Japan. $18-20.

Benjamin Bunny. 3". 1960s. Japan. $18-20.

Brer Fox. 3.5". 1960s. Japan. $18-20.

Mice. 3". 1960s. Japan. $18-20.

Tiggy Winkle. 3". 1960s.
Japan. $18-20.

Tailor Cutter cats. 3.5".
1960s. Japan. $18-20.

Puss in Boots

Long ago there was a miller, who was so poor that at his death he had nothing to leave to poor Jack but Puss. Jack could not help thinking that he had been treated shabbily. But the cat began to speak. "Dear master, don't be downhearted. I will make your fortune for you, if you will buy me a pair of boots, and give me a bag."

Jack had very little money to spare, but he made up his mind to trust him, and so spent all he possessed upon a pair of boots. Puss brought home stores of good food and also kept the King supplied with game.

Then Puss decided his master should be introduced at Court. So he persuaded him to bathe in a river nearby, having heard that the King would be coming by.

Jack stood shivering in the water when the King's carriage appeared in sight. At once Puss began to call out as loudly as he could:

"Help, help! My Lord the Marquis of Carabas is drowning!"

The King put his head out of the coach and, recognizing the cat, ordered his guards to help the Marquis.

While Jack was being taken out of the water, Puss ran to the King and told him that some rogues had run off with his master's clothes while he was bathing, although actually Puss had hidden them under a stone.

On hearing this story, the King ordered one of his grooms to fetch a handsome suit. Jack looked so well that the King and his daughter invited him to their coach.

Meanwhile Puss, who was ahead of the royal party, arrived at a castle which belonged to a cruel Ogre. Puss knocked at the door and asked to see the Ogre, who received him quite civilly.

The Ogre, who was very conceited, began to boast of what clever tricks he could play.

"I have been told," said Puss, "that you possess the power of changing yourself into any kind of animal."

And in a moment a mouse was running about and the Ogre had vanished.

Puss then seized the mouse and ate it up.

So now the cat had a fine castle, and stood at the castle gates to welcome his master and the royal party to a feast.

Puss helped his Majesty to alight, and Jack, or the Marquis as he was now called, gave his hand to the young Princess.

And so the miller's son married the King's daughter.

On the evening of the wedding day a great ball was given. Puss opened the ball, wearing a pair of boots made of the finest leather, with gold tassels and scarlet heels.

3.25". 1960s. Shawnee Pottery. $30-35.

3.25". 1960s. Shawnee Pottery, USA. $18-20.

4.25". 1950s. USA. Probably NEC. $18-20.

2.75". 1960s. Japan. $20-25.

Three piece. 2.5". 1960s. Japan. Note: Boots are the S&P. $45-50.

3.5". 1960s. Japan. $15-18.

2.5". 1980s. Japan. $10-12.

2.5". 1950s. California Creations by Bradley. Japan. $12-15.

2.75". 1960s. Japan. $10-12.

4.25". 1960s. Japan. $20-25.

3.75". 1960s. Japan. $18-20.

The Queen of Hearts

The Queen of Hearts, she made some tarts
All on a summer's day.
The Knave of Hearts, he stole those tarts
And with them ran away.

The King of Hearts called for the tarts
And beat the Knave full sore.
The Knave of Hearts brought back the tarts
And vowed he'd steal no more.

3.25". 1950s. M.Weese, USA. $50-60.

3.5". 1960s. Marked Pack of Cards Series by H.G. Wood, England. Shown with pitcher. $50-60.

4". 1950s. Brayton Laguna Pottery, USA. $125+.

4". 1950s. Japan. $35-40.

Raggedy Ann and Andy

Raggedy Ann and Andy were patented in 1915 by Johnny Gruelle, who was the creator and designer of the dolls. Subsequently several other companies have produced them. Today's version looks quite different from the original creation, which had brown hair made of yarn, oil painted faces, and eyes of wood or tin buttons. From 1928 to 1963 Georgene Novelties produced white versions and Beloved Belindy, a sort of black Raggedy Ann.

3.5". 1960s. Japan. Royal Sealy. $15-20.

4.5". 1940s. USA. Regal China. $70-75.

4". 1990s. China. CIC. $15-18.

4". 1990s. China. CIC. $15-18.

4". 1960s. Japan.
$15-18.

7". 1966. Holt Howard, Japan. $20-25.

3.25". 1970s. Japan. $12-15.

4". 1970s. Private ceramicist, USA. $8-10.

2.75". 1980s. Hong Kong. $5-8.

2.75". 1970s. Probably USA. $10-12.

4.75". 1970s. Japan. Possibly two singles. If pair, $18-20.

2.5". 1960s. © Johnny Gruelle Co, Mfg by Wm. Hirsh Mfg Co, Los Angeles. 4". CA. $40-50.

Rainbow and Pot of Gold

2.5". 1990s.
Indonesia. Enesco.
$15-18.

Miniature. .75". 1960s. USA.
Arcadia Ceramics, CA. $45-50.

The Raven

by Edgar Allan Poe

2.25". USA.
1950s. $55-60.

Robin Hood

The popularity of Robin Hood is due no doubt to the fact that here is a hero who upholds the ideals of fair play, champions the cause of the poor and weak against the tyranny of the wealthy and the mighty, and leads a life in the greenwood which appeals to the enduring belief that the pastoral way of existence is the ideal one. Above all, Robin Hood is a man of action.

He is a folk hero; his feats and adventures have their origins in the popular ballads of the common people. Whether he ever existed is debatable, but exist he does as an ideal of medieval England, a free man in a ruthless world, with a generous sense of humor and a passion for justice.

Robin Hood, Robin Hood,
Is in the mickle wood;
Little John, Little John,
He to the town is gone.

Robin Hood, Robin Hood,
Is telling his beads,
All in the green wood,
Among the green weeds.

Little John, Little John,
If he comes no more,
Robin Hood, Robin Hood,
He will fret full sore.

Friar Tuck

Friar Tuck condiments. 4". Germany. Goebel. First set, 1954, has exposed toes and rare ceramic spoon. $125-150. Second set, 1955, has black shoes and mustard divides at shoulders. $100-125. Third set, 1970s, mustard splits at neck and tray is slightly trimmed. $90-100.

Robin Hood. 4". 1960s. Japan. $28-30.

Friar Tuck sets. 2.5-3". Germany. Goebel. First set, 1954, both same size. $25-35. Second set large and small, 1955. $30-40. Third set large and small on tray, shiny finish on face and hands, 1970s. $40-50.

3". 1957. Goebel, Germany. $55-60.

Friar Tuck. 2.75". Japan. Copies of the 1954 Goebel set. $12-15.

Friar Tuck. 3". Made in the Orient about 1992, no marks but purchased from a Goebel warehouse. Believed to be a trial production to determine if this set could be manufactured more inexpensively than in Germany. $25-30.

Stacking condiment. 5.25". 1950s. Japan. $120-125.

Condiment. 4.5". 1950s. Probably England. $150+.

3.25". 1970s. Japan. $20-22.

2.5". 1970s. Japan. $18-20.

2.25". 1960s. Japan. $15-18.

3". 1970s. Japan. $12-15.

5.75". 1960s. Twin Winton, USA. $30-35.

5.5". 1960s. USA. $20-25.

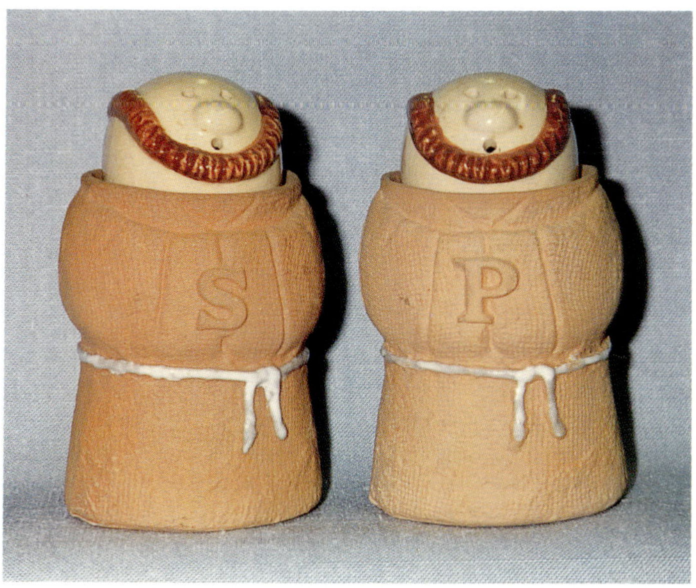

4". 1978. Japan. Enesco. Composition material bottom, ceramic top. $12-15.

The Rooster and the Sun

(Aesop's Fable)

There was once a Rooster who lived in a country in the Far East. Early every morning he crowed loudly, "Cock-a-doodle-do!" And he was sure his crowing was the signal by which the sun rose every day.

With enormous pride he puffed himself out, thinking "How important I am! If it were not for my crowing, the sun would not know when to rise."

One night he decided to find out what would happen if he failed to give the sun his signal. So toward dawn, just before the time when he usually began crowing, he rolled over, shut his eyes, and went to sleep again.

When he awoke there was the sun shining brightly as ever. But the Rooster refused to believe that the sun would have known when to rise without help of some kind from him. "I know what must have happened," he told himself. "Some other Rooster imitated my voice and the sun thought it was my crowing he heard."

Believing one falsehood leads to believing others.

3". 1990s. Clay Art. Philippines. $15-18.

Rooster and sun. 3.75". 1990s. China. Composition material, $8-10.

4". 1990s. China. Strata Group. $15-18.

Rub-a-Dub-Dub

Rub-a-dub dub,
Three men in a tub,
And who do you think they be?
The butcher, the baker,
The candlestick maker;
Turn 'em out, knaves all three!

Rub-a-dub dub,
Three men in a tub,
And how do you think they got there?
The butcher, the baker,
The candlestick maker,
They all jumped out of a rotten potato,
'Twas enough to make a man stare.

It is questionable whether the harmless antics currently attributed to these three characters are the original. In the earliest recordings the rhyme goes:

Hey! rub-a-dub dub, ho! rub-a-dub, three maids in a tub,
And who do you think were there?
The butcher, the baker, the candlestick maker,
All of them gone to the fair.

4.5". 1960s. Japan. Enesco. $65-70.

Sherlock Holmes

Sherlock Holmes & Doctor Watson. 3.75". 1990s. Artone, England. $50-55.

Sherlock Holmes hat and pipe, Detective Mysteries. Mini. 1.25". 1950s. Arcadia Ceramics, USA. $55-60.

Saggy Baggy Elephant

1947 Golden Book by Western Publishing Co.

Sooki the little elephant was walking through the forest and met a parrot. The parrot asked him what kind of an animal he was. When Sooki said an elephant, the parrot told him his ears and nose were too big and his skin way too big for an elephant, and to call himself Saggy Baggy.

2.5". © 1975 Western Publishing Co. Inc. USA. $30-35.

3.25". 1950s. Japan. $35-40.

Sing a Song of Sixpence

Sing a song of sixpence,
A pocket full of rye;
Four-and-twenty blackbirds
Baked in a pie;
When the pie was opened
The birds began to sing;
Wasn't that a dainty dish
To set before the King?
The king was in his counting-house,
Counting out his money;
The queen was in the parlour,
Eating bread and honey.

King and Queen. 3". 1950s. USA. $45-50.

Blackbirds and pie. 2". 1950s. Probably NEC, USA. $25-30.

Swan Song. 2.5". 1970s. USA. $25-30.

Tam O'Shanter & Souter Johnnie from the poem by Robert Burns titled *Tam O'Shanter*. 2.5". 1930s. Germany. Names incised in back of each shaker (although spelling differs some from the poem). $65-75.

The Stork and the Baby

4". 1960s. Japan. Note: each set is a stork with a baby, one a boy and one a girl. $35-40.

Single. 3". 1930s. Goebel, Germany. Incised crown mark. Mate unknown. $90-100.

5". 1980s. Philippines. Vandor, UT. $15-18.

3.75". 1960s. USA. $28-30.

4". 1980s. Sarsaparilla Deco Designs, NJ. $15-18.

Special Delivery. 3.5". 1990s. Philippines. Clay Art. $18-20.

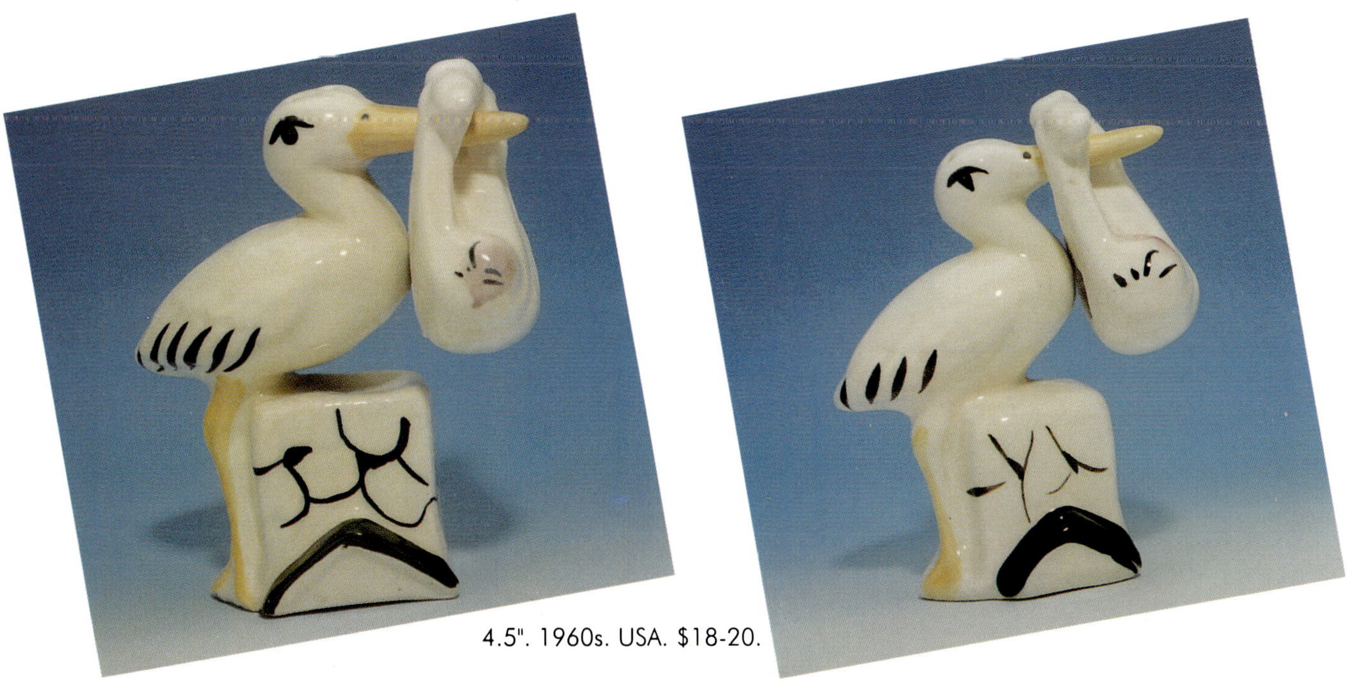

4.5". 1960s. USA. $18-20.

This Little Pig

This little pig went to market,
This little pig stayed at home,
This little pig had roast beef,
This little pig had none,
And this little pig cried, Wee-wee-
wee-wee-wee,
I can't find my way home.

3". 1950s.
Japan. $40-45.

To Market, To Market

To market, to market,
To buy a fat pig,
Home again, home again,
Jiggety jig.
To market, to market,
To buy a fat hog,
Home again, home again,
jiggety-jog.

3.75". 1950s. Japan. Shafford. $30-35.

Tom, Tom, the Piper's Son

Tom, Tom, the piper's son,
Stole a pig and away he did run;
The pig was eat,
And Tom was beat,
And Tom went howling down the street.

2.25". 1950s. Francis Fayre,
England. Single. If pair, $40-45.

Three Little Kittens

Three little kittens, they lost their mittens,
And they began to cry:
"O mother dear,
We very much fear,
That we have lost our mittens."
Lost your mittens!
You naughty kittens!
Then you shall have no pie.

The three little kittens, they found their mittens,
And they began to cry:
"O mother dear,
See here, see here!
See! we have found our mittens."
Put on your mittens
You silly kittens,
And you shall have some pie.

5". 1960s. Japan. Royal Sealy. Note cat on left minus mittens, and end of spoon is a fish. $250+.

Iwo of the three kittens. 3". 1960s. Japan. $22-25.

Two of the three kittens. 4". 1960s. Japan. $55-60.

Tom Sawyer

Tom Sawyer and Huck Finn. 4.5". 1960s. Japan. $75-85.

Tom Sawyer and Becky Thatcher. 2.25". 1950s. USA. $25-30.

Tom Sawyer and fence. 2.5". Huck Finn on raft. 2.75". 1950s. Parkcraft, USA. $45-50.

Treasure Island. 3.5". 1950s. USA. $40-45.

Trolls

Trolls have figured in fairy tales of all types and enthralled children for generations. With few exceptions, trolls have been mean, nasty characters as depicted in Jack Prelutsky's memorable poem *The Troll:*

Beware of the loathsome
troll that slyly lies in wait to
drag you into his dingy hole
and put you on his plate.

3". Japan. 1960s.
Norcrest. $100-125.

Wizard and the dragon. 3.5".
1990s. Philippines. Clay Art.
$18-20.

The Wishing Well and the Garden Gate. 2".
1960s. USA. $30-35.

Unicorns. 3". 1980s.
Taiwan. $8-10.

Series

Condiments with names inscribed on front. 4". 1950s. Shafford. Japan. $125-130.

A Frog he would a-wooing go,
Whether his mother would let him or no.

So off he set with his opera hat,
And on the road he met with a rat.

"Pray, Mr. Rat, will you go with me,"
Kind Mrs. Mousey for to see?"

When they came to the door of Mousey's hall,
They gave a loud knock and they gave a loud call.

"Pray, Mrs. Mouse, are you within?"
"Oh, yes, kind sirs, I'm sitting to spin."

"Pray, Mrs. Mouse, will you give us some beer?
For Froggy and I are fond of good cheer."

"Pray, Mr. Frog, will you give us a song?
But let it be something that's not very long."

"Indeed, Mrs. Mouse," replied the frog.
"A cold has made me as hoarse as a dog."

"Since you have caught cold, Mr. Frog," Mousey said,
"I'll sing you a song that I have just made.

But while they were all a merry-making,
A cat and her kittens came tumbling in.

The cat she seized the rat by the crown;
The kittens they pulled the little mouse down.

This put Mr. Frog in a terrible fright,
He took up his hat, and he wished them good night.

But as Froggy was crossing over a brook,
A lily-white duck came and gobbled him up.

So there was an end of one, two, and three,
The Rat, the Mouse, and the little Frog-gee!

A Frog He Would A-Wooing Go

Old Mother Goose.

Peter Had a Wife

Pussy cat, pussy cat,
Where have you been?
I've been to London
To look at the Queen.
Pussy cat, pussy cat,
What did you there?
I frightened a little mouse
Under her chair.

Pussy Cat, Where have you been?

Stackers with names inscribed on front. 3.5"-4.5". 1950s. Japan. One piece stamped in black, other stamped in green; some are marked Occupied Japan.

Alice in Wonderland $90-100

Little Jack Horner. $40-45.

Bobby Shaftoe's gone to sea,
Silver buckles at his knee;
He'll come back and marry me,
Bonny Bobby Shaftoe.

Bobby Shaftoe's bright and fair,
Combing down his yellow hair,
He's my ain for evermair,
Bonny Bobby Shaftoe.

Bobby Shaftoe's tall and slim,
He's always dressed so neat and trim,
The ladies they all keek at him,
Bonny Bobby Shaftoe.

Bobby Shaftoe's getten a bairn
For to dandle in his arm;
In his arm and on his knee,
Bobby Shaftoe loves me.

Bobby Shaftoe. $40-45.

Old King Cole. $28-30.

Peter, Peter had a Wife. $45-50.

Princess of Thumb. $45-50.

Robin Hood. $28-30.

Robinson Crusoe (from the book by Daniel DeFoe). $30-35.

Poor old Robinson Crusoe!
Poor old Robinson Crusoe!
He made him a coat,
Of an old nanny goat,
What a clever fellow to do so!
With a ring a ting tang,
And a ring a ting tang,
Poor old Robinson Crusoe!

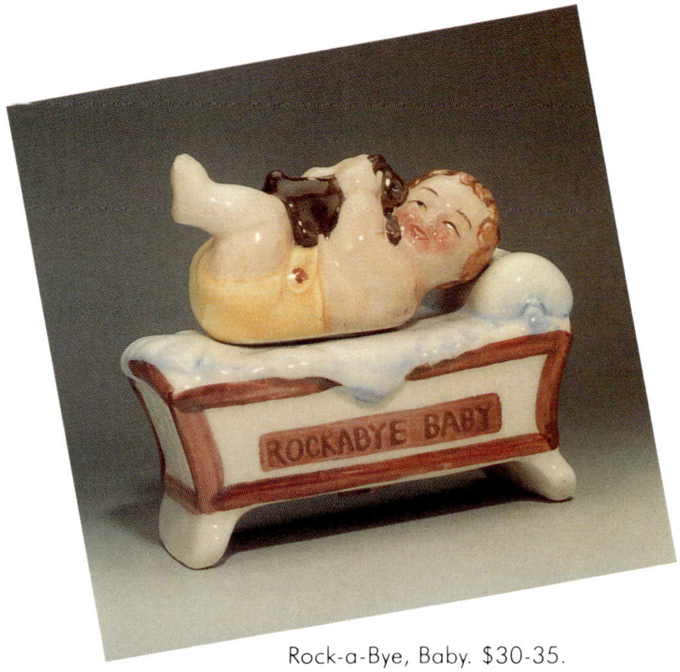

Rock-a-Bye, Baby. $30-35.

Rock-a-bye, baby, thy cradle is green;
Father's a nobleman, mother's a queen;
And Betty's a lady, and wears a gold ring;
And Johnny's a drummer, and drums for the king.

There Was an Old Woman. $35-40.

There was an old woman tossed up in a basket,
Seventeen times as high as the moon;
Where she was going I couldn't but ask it,
For in her hand she carried a broom.
Old woman, old woman, old woman, quoth I,
Where are you going to up so high?
To brush the cobwebs off the sky!
May I go with you? Aye, by-and-by.

Story Book Salts & Peppers by Poinsettia Studios, A Gustin Product, Los Angeles, CA. 2.5"-3.5". 1950s. $70-75.

Top and bottom of original box for Little Miss Muffett.

Little Miss Muffett

Mary Had a Lamb

Peter Peter

Old Mother Hubbard

Old Woman in a Shoe

Wee Willie Winkie runs through the town,
Upstairs and downstairs in his night-gown,
Rapping at the window, crying through the lock,
Are the children all in bed, for now it's eight o'clock?

Wee Willie Winkle

Nursery rhyme series by Relco. 4". 1960s. Japan. $25-28.

Red Riding Hood. Mary had a Little Lamb.

Little Bo Peep and Goldilocks.

Queen of Hearts. Little Miss Muffett.

Storybook Pairs. 3.5". 1989. Taiwan. Danbury Mint. $55-60.

Red Riding Hood and the Wolf. Princess and Frog Prince.

Cinderella and Fairy Godmother. Jack and Jill.

Hansel and Gretel. Tortoise and Hare.

Miniature bone china nursery rhyme series. 2.25". 1960s. Japan. Distributed by Heather House. $90-100.

Cat and the fiddle, and the cow jumped over the moon: Little Jack Horner.

Mary and her lamb. Humpty Dumpty.

Little Miss Muffett. Little Bo Peep.

Little Red Riding Hood and the Wolf. Little Boy Blue and the cow.

The Old Woman in the Shoe. Peter Pumpkin Eater and his wife.

Ol' King Cole and the fiddlers. Jack and Jill.

American Folklore Salt & Pepper Collection. 5.75"-6.25". Sri Lanka. 1994. Issued by Omnibus Division of Fitz & Floyd. $25-30.

Johnny Appleseed, born John Chapman in Massachusetts in 1774. Went West, spreading apple seeds and goodwill.

Paul Bunyan, the legendary lumberjack, with his blue ox "Babe."

Captain Ahab and Moby Dick, the hunter and the hunted in Herman Melville's 1851 novel.

Daniel Boone, American frontiersman. Born 1734. Famous for settlement of Kentucky.

Casey at the bat. In 1888 the *San Francisco Examiner* reported a fictional baseball game. Mudville's favorite slugger struck out, costing his team the game.

Casey Jones. The wreck of the Cannonball Express and the death of its conductor inspired the railway ballad.

Pocahontas, the daughter of a Native American chief, saved the life of Captain John Smith, a Virginia settler.

John Henry was a steel driving man. A worker on the Chesapeake and Ohio Big Bend Tunnel in the 1870s.

Bibliography

Beaupré Miller, Olive, ed. *In the Nursery of my Bookhouse*. The Bookhouse for Children Publishers: Chicago, 1920.

Bookshelf for Boys & Girls, The, Volumes 1-3. The University Society, Inc.: New York, 1960.

Fadiman, Clifton, selected by. *The World Treasury of Children's Literature, Book I.*. Little, Brown and Company: Boston-Toronto, 1984.

Johnson, Sickels, and Sayers. *Anthology of Children's Literature*. Houghton Mifflin Company: Boston, 1970.

Mother Goose's Rhymes, Jingles & Fairy Tales. Henry Altemus Company: Philadelphia, 1896.

O'Connor, Muriel. *Muriel's Character Corner*. Novelty Salt & Pepper Shakers Club newsletter.

Opie, Iona, and Peter Opie, assembled by. *The Oxford Nursery Rhyme Book*. Oxford University Press: London, 1957.

Opie, Iona, and Peter Opie, eds. *The Oxford Dictionary of Nursery Rhymes*. Oxford University Press: London, 1952.

Rinehart, Joyce. "Raggedy Ann Brings Joy to Collectors through the Years." *Antique Trader Weekly*. December 1994.

Vernon Jones, V.S., trans. *Aesop's Fables*. William Heinemann Ltd.: London, 1912.

Index